WORLD CUP HEROES

by Kurt Waldendorf

CAPSTONE PRESS
a capstone imprint

Published by Capstone Press, an imprint of Capstone
1710 Roe Crest Drive, North Mankato, Minnesota 56003
capstonepub.com

Library of Congress Cataloging-in-Publication Data is available on the Library of Congress website

ISBN: 979-8-8752-6973-8 (hardcover)
ISBN: 979-8-8752-6968-4 (paperback)
ISBN: 979-8-8752-6969-1 (ebook PDF)

Summary: All sports have heroes, but soccer heroes are something special. Readers can learn all about the greatest leaders, best teammates, and winningest players to be involved in the planet's greatest game.

Editorial Credits
Editor: Heather Williams; Designer: Cynthia Della-Rovere; Media Researchers: Courtney Rust, Catherine Guden

Image Credits
Getty: Allsport/Hulton Archive, 18, Catherine Ivill, 29, Chris Brunskill/Fantasista, 25, Christof Koepsel/Bongarts, 8, Jamie Squire/Allsport, 14–15, Jed Jacobsohn, 20–21, Jose Breton/Pics Action/NurPhoto, 26, Julian Finley, 5, Maja Hitij, cover (middle), 23, Martin Rose, 10–11, Michael Steele, cover (right), Pictorial Parade/ Archive Photos, 7, Popperfoto, 16–17, Richard Heathcote, 22, Robert Cianflone, 13, Scott Heavey, cover (left), Stu Forster, cover (top)

Design Elements
Shutterstock: Arroyan Art, Dmitry Rukhlenko, Donglpix, madorf, Vector-3D

Printed and bound in China. 6459

CONTENTS

Chapter 1
WHAT MAKES A HERO? 4

Chapter 2
HISTORIC HEROES 6

Chapter 3
HEROIC TEAMS 16

Chapter 4
TODAY'S HEROES 24

GLOSSARY .30
READ MORE .31
INTERNET SITES .31
INDEX .32
ABOUT THE AUTHOR .32

Words in **bold** are in the glossary.

CHAPTER 1

WHAT MAKES A HERO?

Each player uses different skills on the soccer field. Some players are known for their speed. Others are strong shooters. Still others help their team win with great shot-blocking in the net. Whatever their special skill, these star athletes stand out above the rest.

The Men's and Women's World Cups bring together star players from around the world. These tournaments are soccer's biggest events. They give players the chance to become more than stars. By proving their skill against the top **national teams** in the world, players can become heroes of the game.

Lionel Messi (center) is one of the most recognized athletes in the world.

FAST FACT

Hundreds of athletes compete in the Men's and Women's World Cups. Still, these events include only the best of the best. Less than 1 percent of **professional** men's players make the cut. In the women's tournament, less than 4 percent of pros compete.

CHAPTER 2

HISTORIC HEROES

Players can become World Cup heroes in many different ways. But all heroes have one thing in common: they play their best in the biggest moments.

Winners

Some players lead their team to victory over and over. Pelé was only 17 when he helped Brazil win the 1958 Men's World Cup. He went on to lead the team to titles again in 1962 and 1970. "The King" is the only player to win three Men's World Cups.

Kristine Lilly led the U.S. Women's National Team (USWNT) to victory for more than 20 years. Across five Women's World Cups, she won a record 24 matches. The USWNT won two Women's World Cup titles with Lilly on the team.

Pelé (right) was the first teenager to score in a World Cup final. He held the record as Brazil's all-time top goal-scorer for more than 50 years.

Scorers

Some players become heroes by getting the ball into the back of the net. Teams always have a shot with these players on the field.

Marta was the first soccer player ever to score in five different World Cup tournaments.

No player has scored more World Cup goals than Marta. She tallied a whopping 17 goals across five tournaments. In 2007, she scored seven goals in a single Women's World Cup. The mark earned her the Golden Boot, which is given to the tournament's top scorer.

Germany's Miroslav Klose was a strong goal scorer outside of the Men's World Cup. But during the event, he took his game to another level. Across four tournaments, Klose scored a men's record 16 goals.

Tough Competition

Not every top scorer does well at the World Cup. Christine Sinclair of Canada holds the record for **international goals** with 190. Cristiano Ronaldo holds the men's record. He scored 135 for Portugal. But both players struggled at the World Cup, scoring in less than half of their matches.

Abby Wambach celebrates her header goal during the 2011 Women's World Cup.

Game Changers

Soccer is a game of style. Some players make their mark by introducing exciting new ways of playing the game.

Abby Wambach used her head to change the game. The American scored 77 of her 184 international goals on **headers**. Her biggest goal came in a 2011 Women's World Cup match against Brazil. In the final moments, she leaped to connect with a long pass. Her forehead knocked the ball into the net, helping the USWNT advance.

Johan Cruyff of the Netherlands changed the game with his smarts. He helped introduce "total football." The **strategy** allowed players to shift into different roles on the field. Cruyff predicted his teammates' moves, hitting them with precise passes. Cruyff led the Netherlands to the Men's World Cup final in 1974.

Shot Stoppers

Goalkeepers don't often get the attention that scorers do. But sometimes, shot stoppers steal the show. Nadine Angerer did this at the Women's World Cup in 2007. The German faced 31 shots in the tournament. She didn't let any reach the back of the net. Germany coasted to its second Women's World Cup title.

Gianluigi Buffon of Italy had a similar run during the Men's World Cup in 2006. Buffon made 40 saves across seven matches. He gave up only two goals in the tournament. One was knocked in by his teammate. The other was on a **penalty kick**. Buffon's heroic play earned Italy its fourth Men's World Cup title.

U.S. goalkeeper Tim Howard holds the record for most saves in a World Cup match. In 2014, Howard made an amazing 16 saves in a game against Belgium.

During the 2014 World Cup, Tim Howard allowed only six goals in four games.

Sun Wen played for the Chinese soccer team for 13 years. In 2019, she became Vice President of the Chinese Football Association.

Fan Favorites

Not every hero is the biggest or fastest. Not every hero plays for a top team.

Diego Maradona didn't look like most players. He wasn't tall and lanky. But Maradona never stopped moving. He was exciting and emotional. Fans loved watching him play. In 1986, Maradona led Argentina to a Men's World Cup title. Along the way, his joy and persistence made him a fan favorite around the world.

Sun Wen won over fans as an **underdog**. Not many people gave China a chance in the 1999 women's tournament. The USWNT looked unstoppable. Still, Sun rose to the occasion. She led the Chinese team to a tie in the final. The United States won the match in penalty kicks. But Sun earned the Golden Ball, given to the event's top player.

HEROIC TEAMS

During some World Cups, a whole team steps up. They play well throughout the tournament. Some teams even compete for multiple World Cup titles in a row. Brazil, Italy, and Germany have had the most success in the Men's World Cup. In the Women's World Cup, the United States has dominated. Each nation has had heroic teams.

Brazil's National Treasure

Brazil's top team of all time played in the 1970 Men's World Cup. The team was led by Pelé. But the whole **roster** was full of playmakers. In six matches, they racked up 19 goals and allowed only seven. In the final, Brazil breezed past Italy 4–1. The win gave Brazil its third title in four consecutive World Cups. Many consider the team to be the best men's team in history.

Pelé (right) goes in for a tackle against Uruguay's Juan Mujica during the 1970 World Cup.

Franz Beckenbauer (left) shakes hands before a match in the 1974 World Cup. Beckenbauer captained Germany's team to World Cup victory that year.

Germany's Tough Team

Not every top team succeeds right away. That was the case for the German men's team in the 1970s. The team was talented. It was led by stars Franz Beckenbauer and Gerd Müller. But in the 1970 World Cup, the team lost unexpectedly to Italy in the semifinals.

In 1974, Germany got off to a slow start, losing a match in the **group stage**. But the team showed its skill as the event went on. In the final, Germany faced Johan Cruyff and the Netherlands. It was a difficult test. The Dutch jumped out to a lead. They scored in the second minute. Eventually, Germany came back to win 2–1. The team's persistence and strength against great competition made them World Cup heroes.

Defender Franz Beckenbauer showed his toughness during the 1970 tournament. In the match against Italy, he hurt his shoulder badly. Still, he played out the match with his arm in a sling.

Early U.S. Women's Success

The USWNT's success started early. At the first Women's World Cup in 1991, the team scored an outstanding 25 goals. They gave up only five on their way to their first title. Four years later, the team played well again. But the United States took a disappointing third place.

In 1999, the Americans got back on track. The team swept through the group stage, scoring 13 goals and giving up only one. The final match was against China. About 90,000 fans cheered from the stands. The United States won a dramatic victory during penalty kicks. The match made Michelle Akers, Mia Hamm, and Brandi Chastain familiar names around the world. It also made the '99ers World Cup heroes.

Mia Hamm and the 1999 USWNT helped make soccer popular in the United States with their World Cup win.

Alex Morgan (left) and Megan Rapinoe (right) celebrate Rapinoe's goal against the Netherlands during the 2019 World Cup final.

A New Generation

Players who grew up admiring the '99ers took the stage in the 2010s. The team's success started in 2011. The USWNT finished in a close second to Japan. Four years later, the USWNT got revenge. They beat Japan 5–2 in the 2015 final.

But the best was yet to come. In 2019, the USWNT finished their dominant decade. They beat the Netherlands to capture their second straight title. The team won all seven matches in the tournament. They scored a record 26 goals. Americans Alex Morgan and Megan Rapinoe tied for most goals with six. And Rapinoe earned the Golden Ball. The squad is thought by many to be the top women's team of all time.

Crystal Dunn takes a shot during the 2019 World Cup.

TODAY'S HEROES

In recent years, new players have become World Cup heroes. Others have become stars to watch.

Men's Heroes

Kylian Mbappé and Olivier Giroud were rising stars in 2018. The pair helped lead France to the Men's World Cup title. In 2022, they shone again. Giroud knocked in a game-winner against England in the quarterfinals. In the final against Argentina, Mbappé scored three goals, tying a record set in 1966. France lost the match. But Mbappé took home the Golden Boot as the tournament's top scorer. Giroud was tied for third-most goals in the tournament.

In 2018, Kylian Mbappé became only the second teenager in history to score in a World Cup final.

Lionel Messi

Argentina's Lionel Messi has had many heroic moments. Messi has played in more Men's World Cup matches than any other player. He ranks second in men's international goals. In 2022, Messi added the one accomplishment he was missing. He led Argentina to a World Cup title. Messi scored twice in the final against France.

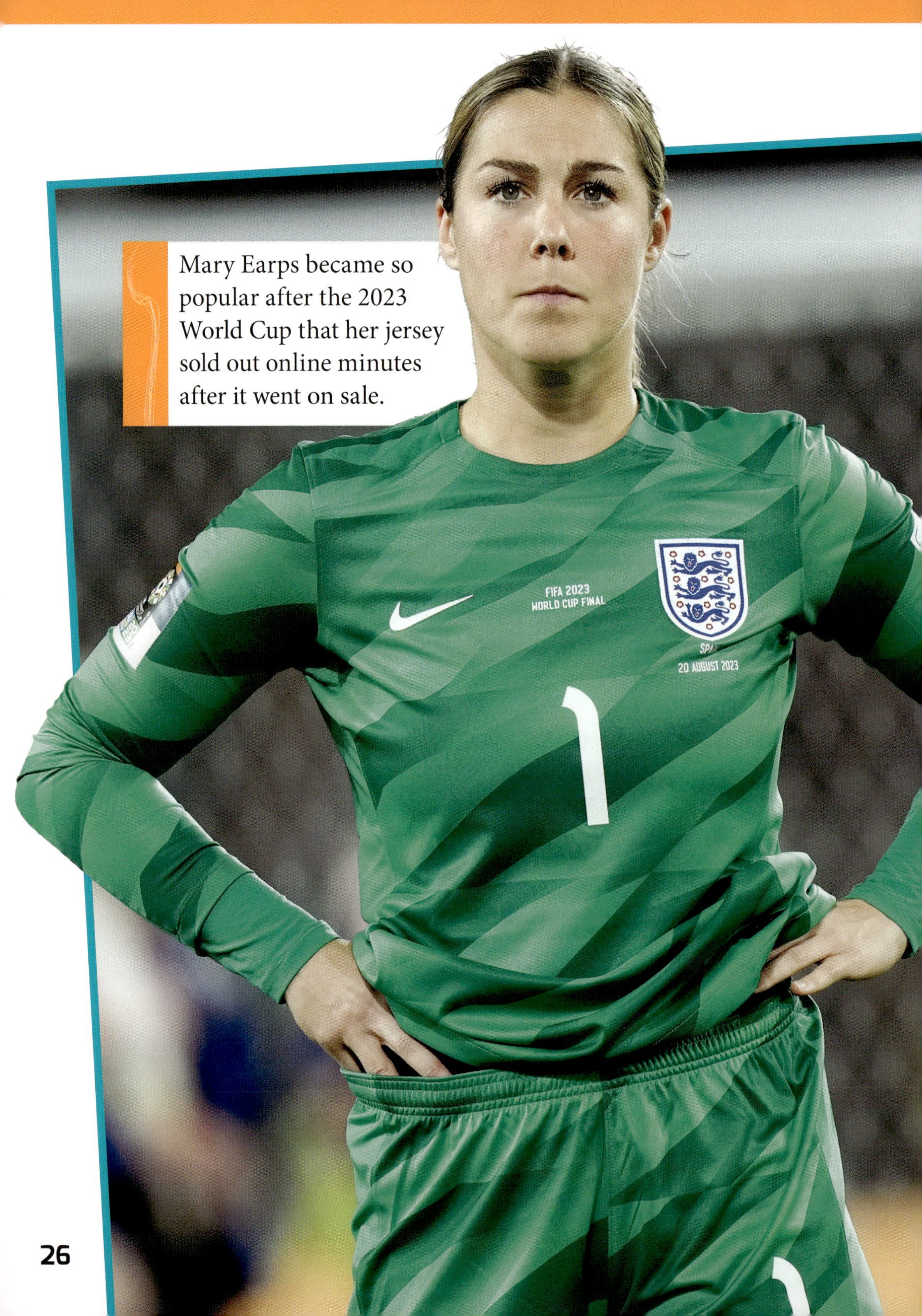

Mary Earps became so popular after the 2023 World Cup that her jersey sold out online minutes after it went on sale.

Women's Heroes

A pair of heroes stepped up during the 2023 Women's World Cup: goaltender Mary Earps and midfielder Aitana Bonmatí.

Earps was in the net for every minute of England's matches. She allowed just four goals throughout the tournament. Her biggest moment came in the final. Earps dove to save a hard penalty kick by Spain. Although they lost the final and came in second, her quick **reflexes** helped England to its best-ever finish at the World Cup. It also earned her the Golden Glove for top keeper at the tournament.

Bonmatí was part of the high-powered Spanish team. The squad scored 18 goals and gave up only seven. Bonmatí was a big reason for this. She was one of Spain's top scorers and had two assists. After beating Earps and England 1–0 in the final, Spain took home its first Women's World Cup title. Bonmatí earned the Golden Ball for her performance.

Future Heroes

New stars step up at each World Cup. Sometimes these performances are surprises. But often players build success for many years beforehand.

Enzo Fernández showed his skill at the Men's World Cup in 2022. The young midfielder helped Argentina take the title. He was named the event's Best Young Player. Norway's Erling Haaland has also stood out. At the age of 24, Haaland became his country's top international goal scorer. Although Norway didn't qualify for the Men's World Cup in 2022, fans hoped Haaland would help the team make it to the 2026 tournament.

Salma Paralluelo of Spain and Sophia Smith of the United States are rising women's stars. Paralluelo was just 19 when she was named Best Young Player at the 2023 Women's World Cup. Even though the USWNT lost in the Round of 16 during the 2023 World Cup, Smith scored the team's first goal of the tournament. She has also found success away from the World Cup. In 2024, she helped her country take gold at the Olympic Games. Fans grew excited about Smith's potential as a World Cup hero.

Each generation has star players. By proving their skill against one another on the biggest stage, a select few will become World Cup heroes.

Thanks to Salma Paralluelo's game-winning goal in the quarterfinals, Spain moved on and eventually won the 2023 World Cup.

GLOSSARY

group stage (GROOP STAYJ)—part of a tournament in which teams play multiple matches against a small set of competitors

headers (HED-urz)—shots or passes where players use their heads to hit the ball

international goals (in-tur-NASH-uh-nuhl GOALZ)—scoring plays that count for a country's national team

national teams (NASH-uh-nuhl TEEMZ)—sports squads that represent their countries

penalty kick (PEN-uhl-tee KICK)—a free kick awarded to the offense when the defense commits a penalty

professional (pruh-FESH-uh-nuhl)—engaged in by people who receive money for what they do

reflexes (REE-flek-sez)—a person's ability to react quickly

roster (ROSS-tur)—a list of people on a team

strategy (STRAT-uh-jee)—a plan for winning a game or contest

underdog (UHN-der-dawg)—a person or team that is not expected to win an event

READ MORE

Chandler, Matt. *Featuring Lionel Messi: Facts, Quizzes, Activities, and More!* North Mankato, MN: Capstone, 2026.

Flynn, Brendan. *The World Soccer Encyclopedia.* Minneapolis: ABDO, 2025.

Marthaler, Jon. *The Best Teams of World Soccer.* Minneapolis: ABDO, 2024.

INTERNET SITES

Britannica Kids: Women's World Cup
kids.britannica.com/kids/article/Womens-World-Cup/638782

Britannica Kids: World Cup
kids.britannica.com/kids/article/World-Cup/390872

ESPN: World Cup
www.espn.com/soccer/league/_/name/fifa.world

TIME for Kids: World Cup Win
www.timeforkids.com/g34/world-cup-win/

U.S. Soccer
www.ussoccer.com/

INDEX

Akers, Michelle, 20
Angerer, Nadine, 12

Beckenbauer, Franz, 19
Bonmatí, Aitana, 27
Buffon, Gianluigi, 12

Chastain, Brandi, 20
Cruyff, Johan, 11, 19

Earps, Mary, 27

Fernández, Enzo, 28

Giroud, Olivier, 24

Haaland, Erling, 28
Hamm, Mia, 20
Howard, Tim, 12

Klose, Miroslav, 9

Lilly, Kristine, 6

Maradona, Diego, 15
Marta, 9
Mbappé, Kylian, 24
Messi, Lionel, 25
Morgan, Alex, 23
Müller, Gerd, 19

Netherlands, 11, 19, 23

Paralluelo, Salma, 28
Pelé, 6, 16

Rapinoe, Megan, 23
Ronaldo, Cristiano, 9

Sinclair, Christine, 9
Smith, Sophia, 28
Sun Wen, 15

Wambach, Abby, 10

About the Author

Kurt Waldendorf is the author of more than a dozen books for children. When he's not writing or editing, he enjoys indoor rock climbing and running along the shore of Lake Michigan with his dog. He lives in Chicago.